GOD IS IN LOVE WITH A PREGNANT GIRL

What kind of love is this?

Linda Reece

Gotham Books

30 N Gould St.
Ste. 20820, Sheridan, WY 82801
https://gothambooksinc.com/

Phone: 1 (307) 464-7800

© 2025 *Linda Reece*. All rights reserved.

No part of this book may be reproduced, stored in a retrieval system, or transmitted by any means without the written permission of the author.

Published by Gotham Books (January 28, 2025)

ISBN: 979-8-3481-1183-0 (P)
ISBN: 979-8-3481-1185-4 (E)

Because of the dynamic nature of the Internet, any web addresses or links contained in this book may have changed since publication and may no longer be valid.

The views expressed in this work are solely those of the author and do not necessarily reflect the views of the publisher, and the publisher hereby disclaims any responsibility for them.

"Behold, I am the LORD, *the* God *of all flesh:* is there anything too hard *for me?"*

- Jeremiah 32:27

Contents

1. Stomach Ache 1
    Introduction 6
2. Bath Tub 8
3. You're Going To Jail 12
4. Never Depart From It 17
5. The Swords 21
6. Many Waters 29
7. Tree Uproot 36
8. Georgia State University/The Flood Waters 41
9. Ball of Fire 46
10. Symphony of The Psalms 51
11. Name The Child 55
12. I Am With Thee Always 59

ENCOUNTER #1

STOMACH ACHE

I lived in the projects in Cincinnati, Ohio with my mom, dad, sister and three brothers. My dad was a spiritual man. He taught me regularly about the Bible. The study of it was his passion. Dad described the love that Jesus had for us, so much so that he died for us. He told me how Jesus would come whenever I needed him and how he would answer my prayers. About five-years old, Dad began sitting me down, reading the Bible to me and explaining certain passages. I became fascinated with Jesus Christ and the Bible. From Genesis, dad showed me the sin and rebellion of man that took place in the Garden of Eden. He explained how the entire human race needed God's forgiveness because of Adam and Eve's disobedience. One of my dad's favorite scriptures was John 3:16. I memorized it very early. Dad enlightened me on the importance of having love one towards another and having faith in God. He wanted to make sure our family would one day be together again in heaven. This Jesus amazed me! I mean, just think about Him. He has no beginning. He has no ending. He spoke and everything was. At his command everything came into existence. He even died, but death couldn't stop him. He came back! Wow! The more my dad taught me about the Bible, the more I began to love the

God of the Bible. To think that God made the clouds, rivers, birds, the sun, and all of us, was just really, really big! I mean, just beyond incredible! In my eyes, God was the greatest phenomenon to ever exist and that will ever exist! I would sometimes urge my dad to tell me more about Jesus.

One afternoon, I was upstairs in my sister's and my bedroom. She was not home at the time, nor were my two older brothers. Dad was downstairs in his favorite chair watching television. My mom also was downstairs tending to my baby brother of just a few months old. I was eight-years old when something extraordinary happened.

Out of nowhere, a sharp constant pain gripped my stomach to the point where I could barely move or even speak above a whisper. It was strange that pain of that magnitude came upon me so suddenly and at the level that it did. I first gently rocked back and forth tightly hugging my waist. I began to cry, groaning softly. What was this? I thought if I could just get downstairs to my dad, he would know what to do. Slowly, I rolled off my twin bed onto the floor. My legs were drawn into a fetal position. The excruciating pain felt like a knife was lodged in my belly that locked me into place. I was completely unable to move. Dad was only a few feet away, if only I could get to him or call for him. I desperately wanted him to come help me. I thought I was dying. What could I do? There was no one to help me. But then, I remembered dad telling me to call on Jesus if I was ever afraid or in trouble. I counted on that being true right then. He was my only hope. Through soft lamentation, I faintly whispered, "It hurts Jesus! I'm scared! Please help me, Jesus! Daddy said you would. Please make my stomach feel better." Within mere seconds of my request, I was released from the clutch of pain. It was more like jerked loosed from the gripping agony which held my body drawn inward. The pain left me immediately and completely! Vanished! Gone! It was as if Jesus snapped his fingers, and it was done! I was totally amazed! Glee filled my heart! My pain did leave when I called on the Name of Jesus! He really heard me! I cried tears of joy! He helped me! It was true! It was really true that Jesus will answer when we call!

Totally ecstatic, I got up, ran downstairs, and jumped into my dad's lap. I told him everything that happened. Holding me closely, he rejoiced! Tears of joy filled his eyes.

"Praise the Lord!" He said softly.

"Always remember what Jesus did for you today, honey." He continued tenderly.

"Always remember this. He will never leave you or forget about you."

"I will. Dad! I think God likes me!"

He chuckled. "Yes baby, I think he does."

From that day on I wanted to know everything I could about the Lord Jesus Christ! Now, it wasn't just dad teaching me about Jesus. I had experienced him for myself! And like my dad, I know Jesus Christ is real and that he is a very present help in the time of trouble. He is no respect of persons. What he did for me, he will do for you. Call on him with the believing heart of a child and he will come to you. He will. He really will!

> "...Except ye be converted, and become as little children, ye shall not enter into the kingdom of heaven."
>
> *Matthew 18:3*

ME & MY SISTER'S ROOM
JESUS PLEASE MAKE MY STOMACH STOP HURTING. DADDY SAID YOU WOULD HELP ME WHEN I ASK YOU. HELP ME, JESUS.
WAH! WAH!
DADDY! DADDY! JESUS MADE MY STOMACH FEEL BETTER!

INTRODUCTION

<u>The Definition of a Miracle</u>:

A surprising and welcome event that is not explicable by natural or scientific laws and is therefore considered to be the work of a divine agency.

<u>The Definition of Sovereign</u>:

Possessing supreme or ultimate power.

<u>Synonyms of sovereign</u>:

Supreme, Absolute, Unlimited, Unrestricted, Unrestrained, Boundless, Infinite, Total, Paramount, Unconditional, Principal, Chief, Dominate, Ruling, Royal, Regal, Kingly, Monarchical.

Many don't believe in the miraculous things the Lord can and will do for those whom he chooses. I do believe that because the Heavenly Father has graced me to experience several of them, miracles that is. I am humbled to think the God of all there is chose me to bestow such incredible encounters. I pray you will find hope and encouragement through these supernatural testimonials.

I ask the Lord to help you to know that he loves you unconditionally. He is available to you. All you need to do is repent, which means turn from sin. Turn the direction of your life over to the Lord Jesus Christ. Ask him to be Lord and Savior of your life and he will. He knows how tired you are of doing whatever it is that keeps you separated from him. He knows of your need for freedom from sin, which is why he died for you. A blood debt was owed for sin.

> *"...and without the shedding of blood, there is no remission (forgiveness)."*
>
> *Hebrews 9:22*

We are all guilty of transgression of his laws. But his love for us brought him to us in human form to pay that debt for us in full on the cross. His death freed you and me. He died so you and I could live eternally with him. Through him, you can be relieved of the heavy load of sin and the guilt it carries. Ask his forgiveness. He loves you beyond what you can imagine. Call on him. Cry out to him. He knows your name.

ENCOUNTER #2

BATH TUB

Although the healing of my stomach would never be forgotten, my attention, as I became a teenager, had taken a rebellious turn.

Dad was a strict disciplinarian. About age 15, I started not to like him very much. I respected and loved him, but he wouldn't allow me the freedom to do what I wanted (Duh). He was a parent). So, he lost major brownie points in my book.

We moved from the projects in the city to a three-bedroom house in the suburbs. I was enrolled in a new middle school where I met new friends. These were pot smoking, alcohol drinking, class skipping friends and I joined right in. Even though I drank alcohol, smoked pot, and sometimes skipped classes, I would often leave my company of friends to frequent the school library. There, I read fascinating books on philosophy and religion. I still wanted to know more about God than just what Dad had taught me. I wanted to know him personally. Things like, where was he? Is Jesus God? What about his death on the cross? The resurrection? Could I see him? Could I talk to him? Will he talk to me? Could I touch

Him? I wanted to know all these things, but meanwhile I remained on a rebellious path.

One Friday afternoon, I rushed home after school to finish my chores. My friends were waiting outside in our driveway for me to finish. My dad was so stern they preferred not to be in his presence. They waited outside. However, we were all anxious to "cop" a bag of marijuana and just hang out. Once that was accomplished, we would have to decide which one of us would steal our parents' car for a short, fun, joyride. Yeah, we were pretty horrible.

I hurriedly cleaned the bathroom. I was scrubbing the tub. My dad sat in the den directly across the hall from the bathroom where he watched television, his favorite past time when he wasn't working at the Post Office.

I was stretched over the tub scouring the back of it. When suddenly I heard an audible voice calling me that I thought could have been my dad.

"Linda."

I pulled myself up from the tub and leaned forward to look across the hall. My dad was not looking in my direction, but continued uninterrupted, watching television.

That's odd. I thought. But ok, whatever.

It was back to scrubbing the tub. After all, weed and happy times awaited me. Again, I hear my name called, "Linda."

But this time the distinct, clear voice resonated within my spirit as being God himself! He speaks in many ways. You may ask how did I know it was God? There is feature that God placed within every human being that has the capability to recognize his voice. It's like no other. His voice transcends the mind and soul. It speaks directly to the human spirit. His voice has a lean, tender sound. The sound as of the only all wise God who changes not. It was totally incredible! It was God! The King of Kings! He called my name! Twice! Again, I pulled myself up from the tub, whipped around and sat on its side. With a bowed head, I quietly waited in awe, wondering what he might say to me. About a second passed, he did speak to my spirit saying, "I want you to serve me."

Somehow, I was not afraid. On the contrary, I felt totally comfortable when I replied. Like a child speaking to a father, I answered, "Ok. If you teach me how."

After that, I proceeded with my crazy plans with friends. But I hid the encounter in my heart.

This meeting answered my questions of will he speak to me? Can talk to him? He is no respect of persons. He will also speak to you. And you can converse with him. As I remember this encounter, I ask myself what did he possibly see in me? What did he want with me? Why would he want a rebellious, disobedient to parents, pot-smoking, alcohol drinker to serve him? It's because his love for us passes knowledge.

I'll say that again. His love for us passes knowledge. What kind of God is this who is mindful of man? Of you? Me? I don't know why he loves us so much. I'm just so glad he does!

> "...and to know the love of Christ which passeth knowledge, that ye might be filled with all the fullness of God.
>
> Ephesians 3:19

> "How precious also are thy thoughts unto me, O God! How great is the sum of them! If I should count them, they are more in number than the sand: when I awake, I am still with thee."
>
> Psalms 139: 17 & 18

ENCOUNTER #3

YOU'RE GOING TO JAIL

Now, I'm eighteen years-old with a one-year-old baby girl. Unfortunately, I was still quite the numbskull. My beautiful little girl meant the world to me. But I was very naïve and still trying to figure stuff out. After graduating high school, I continued hanging out with those same old high school friends. We had added retail store theft to the rebellion list. We stole clothes from stores, ate in restaurants and ran out when our waitress took dishes to the back.

But this particular time, I was alone in a well-known retail store where I picked up an astrology book. I began reading about my zodiac sign. The book intrigued me. Obviously, the author did not know me personally, but the book seemed to portray me to a tee. I was blown away by the accuracy of my described personality. I wanted to take it home and finish reading. But there was one problem, I didn't have any money. So, I got the lovely idea to tuck it into my jacket pocket and casually head towards the exit door. Before I reached the exit, a man placed his hand on my shoulder.

"I'd like to have that book." He said.

I was completely terrified. In total shock, I gazed pitifully at him like a puppy hoping not to get a spanking for pooping on the carpet. I slowly removed the book from my pocket and handed it to him. What a stupid thing I had done. He took me under one arm and ushered me to an office in the back of the store. There he interrogated me. I started balling. Ignoring my tears, he ridiculed me.

"S-o-o-o, you're into astrology. What sign are you?"

I kept silent. I just sat there whimpering, completely horrified.

"Well, let's see what your horoscope says for today." He flipped through the pages.

"Ah! Well, if you're a Scorpio, it says here that you're going to have a very disturbing day. I'd say that's about right, wouldn't you?"

Now, I'm literally trembling with fear.

"Here's one! Aries says this day will not be what you expect? Hmm…I guess there is something to this stuff!"

He called my parents who were instructed to meet me at the police station. I was handcuffed and put in back of a police car.

It felt surreal. In the elevator at the city jail, still handcuffed, the huge Caucasian officer said to me, "If you try anything, I will blow your effing head off!"

I nearly peed my pants. At the jail, I was issued a court date and was free to go home with my parents. I was so happy to see my daughter. Of course, now I called on the Lord for mercy. I had hoped the One who called my name while I was cleaning the bathtub, would spare me any jail time. My parents were terribly disappointed. Dad scolded me but continued teaching me the Holy Scriptures. On the night before my court date, my mom took me to visit Ms. Esther, one of her Christian friends. She was heavily committed the Lord and his Word. She prayed for me and even anointed my head with oil. When mom and I returned home that night, I got on my knees and asked God once again for his mercy the next day. He spoke to my spirit saying these words, "You are going to jail for a short time. You will not be harmed."

Still quite nervous, I did not sleep that night. At court the next day, the judge sentenced me to ten days in the county jail. I turned and looked at my parents who were heartbroken. The bailiff guided me out of the courtroom and later into a patty wagon with other criminals. I was completely mortified. It was obvious that I had never been in situation like that before. An African American male in the wagon taunted me.

"Hey! Mary Poppins! What did you do? Pour too much syrup on your pancakes?" He said and burst into a crazed laughter. I just looked away, petrified.

I took it that was not his first time going to jail.

I was processed in the jail. The ten-day sentence went exactly as the Lord said. I was there for a short time and no one bothered me. It was like I was invisible to the other inmates. No one said anything to me. I did not realize it at the time, but the Lord was shaping me to become more like him. And trust me, there was a whole lot more shaping to be done. Much more. He was chipping away at the dirt so the diamond underneath could shine.

The brief stay in the county jail cured me of stealing, period. Oftentimes, God will allow certain situations to get our attention, so that we call on him. It does not seem pleasant at the time, and no one enjoys trials and tribulations, but even those situations are demonstrations of his tender mercies. God knows all about our sin, frailties, shortcomings, and yet he died for us anyway. That's love.

"But God commendeth his love towards us, in that, while we were yet sinners, Christ died for us."

Romans 5:8

ENCOUNTER #4

NEVER DEPART FROM IT

I had gotten my own apartment for my daughter and me. My dad worked the 11:00 pm – 7:00 a.m. graveyard shift at the Post Office. He stopped by my place every morning to share with me the Holy Bible. Perhaps, after my jail time, he felt I needed more scriptural teaching. I certainly did need it, but I could not comprehend it. There was a whole lot to it, it seemed.

After a couple weeks of his visitations and the teachings, I confessed to him that I did not understand what he was talking about. There was this great peace and humility that emanated from him. He was gentle, loving and kind. Everyone recognized that there was something special about my dad. It was evident to me that he had a relationship with God. I wanted what he had. I wanted to be close to God like that. At times, I was afraid of my dad. When I lived with my parents, I would come home after doing something ungodly, take one glance at him and quickly dismiss myself from his presence. I couldn't even look at him. It was as though he could see right through me. Watching him, I believed God was real, but where was God? How could I find him? How could I really know that the Bible was the absolute truth. I just didn't get it. Hearing my frustration, my dad offered a suggestion.

"Tell you what, honey." He said lovingly.

"Pray. Ask God with your whole heart if the Bible is true and if what I'm teaching you is true. And he will let you know."

I sincerely wanted to know God, so I did exactly what dad said. I prayed every night seeking answers. After about three weeks and having not received an answer, my praying about it fell off. I just stopped praying. Then one morning around dusk maybe, somewhere between 5:00 - 5:30 a.m., the unmistakable presence of God entered my bedroom. Initially, I was scared beyond measure. There was no audible voice. But as I mentioned before, we are constructed to hear him when he speaks to us. He built us to have a means with which to communicate with him if and when we sincerely desire to. I knew it was him. His Spirit spoke to my inner spirit saying, "Fear not."

At his command my entire being, mind, body and soul, became completely relaxed. I felt as though I was on a padded piece of wood, floating tranquilly down a calm river or perhaps flying peacefully on a small slice of carpet. Once relaxed, he again spoke saying,

"What he is telling you is true. Never depart from it."

His presence then lifted away. I was utterly blown away! My God! He actually came to me and answered my prayer! God himself came to me! This is why I can never leave Jesus Christ and the God of the Holy Bible. God made sure of that by telling me himself what the truth really is. He is the truth. His Word is truth. My journey had only just begun. But now, my faith was chosen and sure. At the bath tub, I asked him to teach me how to serve him. He is doing it. And yet still a long road ahead.

I shared this with my dad that morning when he came to visit. He hugged me as tears of joy again streamed down his face. A year later, I moved to Georgia.

Ask him whatever you need to know. Ask sincerely, with no preconceived ideas. Be open to what he may tell you. Ask innocently, like a child. Be thirsty for him. He will answer. It's not about being perfect. It's about having a relationship with him. Humble yourself and have a willing heart to do as his Word commands. It's about repentance, asking for forgiveness and turning away from the sin in your life. It's about receiving Jesus Christ into your hearts as not only Savior, but Lord as well. He offers you the amazing gift of eternal life!

> *"Ask and ye shall receive. Seek and ye shall find. Knock and the door shall be opened unto you."*
>
> Matthew 7:7

> *"My sheep hear my voice, and I know them, and they follow me: And I give unto them eternal life; and they shall never perish, neither shall any man pluck them out of my hand."*
>
> John 10:27 & 28

Wow! Eternal life! There is no better gift!

ENCOUNTER #5

THE SWORDS

In Georgia, I was now six months pregnant with my second child. Times were extremely hard. I was poverty-stricken, severely depressed, confused, afraid. My life was like a fox, wandering around in the woods, who got pulled up in a hunter's net and kept fighting to free itself, but could not. I had no more fight in me. I needed a break from continuous hardships. I needed my mom and dad. I had no other recourse but to temporarily leave Georgia and returned to my parent's home in Ohio. Dad picked up my daughter and me from the bus station. I was the prodigal daughter indeed. In spite of my sin and hard times, I praised God and read the Bible every single day. It was mind blowing that God was with me in the midst of the state of my life. There was a lot I still did not know or understand, but I was sure of one thing, that he was and is *Jehovah Shammah, The Lord is there*. I relied on him to help me figure things out. I needed him to help ground me, so that I was not constantly teetering in life. That stability was yet in the far distance.

I was in the house of the Lord every time the doors opened, literally. God was always on my mind and in my heart. I believed that one day things would get better for my children and me. God was all I knew. He was all I had. And even if things didn't improve, I knew my God was able. I also knew that I would one day I would gain victory over my flesh.

I honored Jesus Christ even when we didn't have enough. I praised Him through my tears when the lights were turned off and we were in the dark, with very little to eat. When we were cold or without water and heat, I exalted my King. My circumstances did not change who he is, his eternal status or reduce the fact that he is still the God of all creation and worthy to be worshipped.

Again, tears streamed down my dad's face when he saw us walking towards him in the bus station. He held me so tightly. He was joyful to see us coming home. But I know he was terribly saddened by our struggle that clearly shown in our tattered appearance. Once we arrived home, Mom heard us getting out of the car in the driveway. She welcomed us from the opened screened door. Over the weeks, I had some great talks with them. They knew I had gone through a lot, but they also knew my faith in God was strong.

Mom and I were at the kitchen table having a delightful conversation over a cup of tea, when suddenly the enemy viciously attacked my mind. He hurled rapid, consecutive, railing accusations.

"You're pathetic! You're nothing! God doesn't love you! Look at you! Whore! You're useless! And you call yourself a Christian! Kill yourself!"

Sitting there with my mom, my countenance changed from one of peace and joy to one of extreme seriousness. Instantly, I went into spiritual battle mode. Slowly, I arose from the table.

"Honey, are you alright?" My mom asked concerned.

I opened the basement door. Without looking back at her I replied, "It's ok, mom. I'll be back."

I shut the door behind me. In the dark I started carefully down the stairs. I began hearing demonic chanting. Yes, I had my issues, but I was a child of the Most-High, God! I was spiritually insulted and angry at the enemy for his audacity of the onslaught. In the Name of Jesus, empowered by the Holy Spirit, I took a defensive and fearless stance. With authority of the Spirit of God, anointed by him with purpose and power for this attack, I pulled forth the sword of the Spirit, which is the Word of God and began my counter attack!

"The Lord is my Shepherd." I said deliberately calculating my first step.

"I shall not want." Carefully stepping yet down another step.

"He maketh me to lie down in green pastures."

Taking still another step, and another. I had reached the bottom of the stairs declaring firmly,

"Yea, though I walk through the valley of shadow death, I will fear no evil for thou art with me..."

Upon saying that, the Lord suspended my outer man, my flesh. It remained still, while my spirit took the forefront position of my being. There, I was given by God, the ability to see in the spirit.

In the spirit, I saw three swords emerge from my mouth. The swords made a swishing sound with each swift and precise hard rotation.

Swoosh! Swoosh! Swoosh! They were cutting the power of demonic forces. I stood there frozen! I witnessed actual warfare in the spirit! I witnessed the power of God, that we as his children have over the enemy through the Word of God! The chanting volume lessened lower and lower until finally it subsided altogether. The accusations ceased. In awe, I felt my way over to the sofa where I sat with raised hands, crying and praising God profusely. Unexpectedly, fluent tongues burst from my mouth! The Word of God is truly alive! What an unimaginable experience! There is great, great, great power in the Word of God!

Look at the condition of my life. And yet he allowed me to participate in something as divine as this! Some may say that God would never show an unwedded pregnant girl, who struggles with fornication, something this supernatural and powerful. And I would reply to them, God is sovereign! "For my thoughts are not your thoughts. Neither are your ways my ways, saith the Lord." Isaiah 55:8

It's not about where we are in life that determines his love for us or whether he will share great things with us. It's do we have a relationship with him. He simply wants to be our Father and us to be his children. Talk to him. Rely on him. Believe in him. He wants us to trust him wholly.

This Scripture comes to mind regarding this encounter:

"For the word of God is quick, and powerful and sharper than any two-edged sword…"

Hebrews 4:12

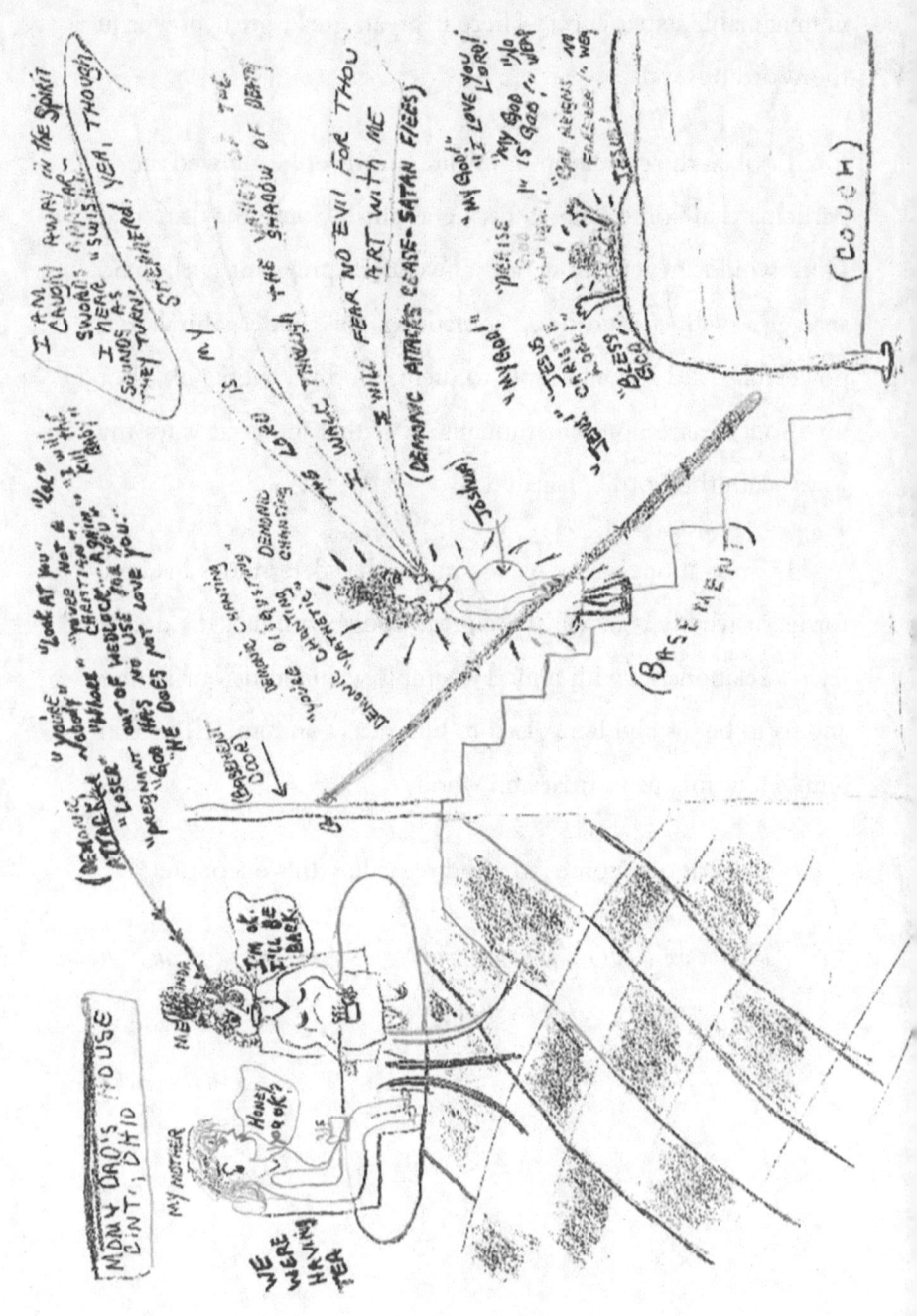

The Word of God dismantled the attack. The Word of God is living and powerful! God is real! His Word is real, authoritative, absolute and true! Mom was still sitting at the kitchen table when I returned upstairs. Surely, my countenance was different when I opened the basement door.

Astonished, she asked, "Linda! Honey, is everything okay?"

I did not explain. She would not have understood at that time. On the contrary, she may have thought I was crazy, like some of you are thinking right now. I teared up, closed my eyes, raised both hands high and shouted, "Praise God Almighty! It is well with my soul! It is well with my soul!"

Friends, read the Bible. Know Scripture. Believe it. Study it. Meditate on it. Embrace it. Fall in love with it.

"Not withstanding in this rejoice not that the spirits are subject unto to you, but rather rejoice because your names are written in heaven."

Luke 10:20

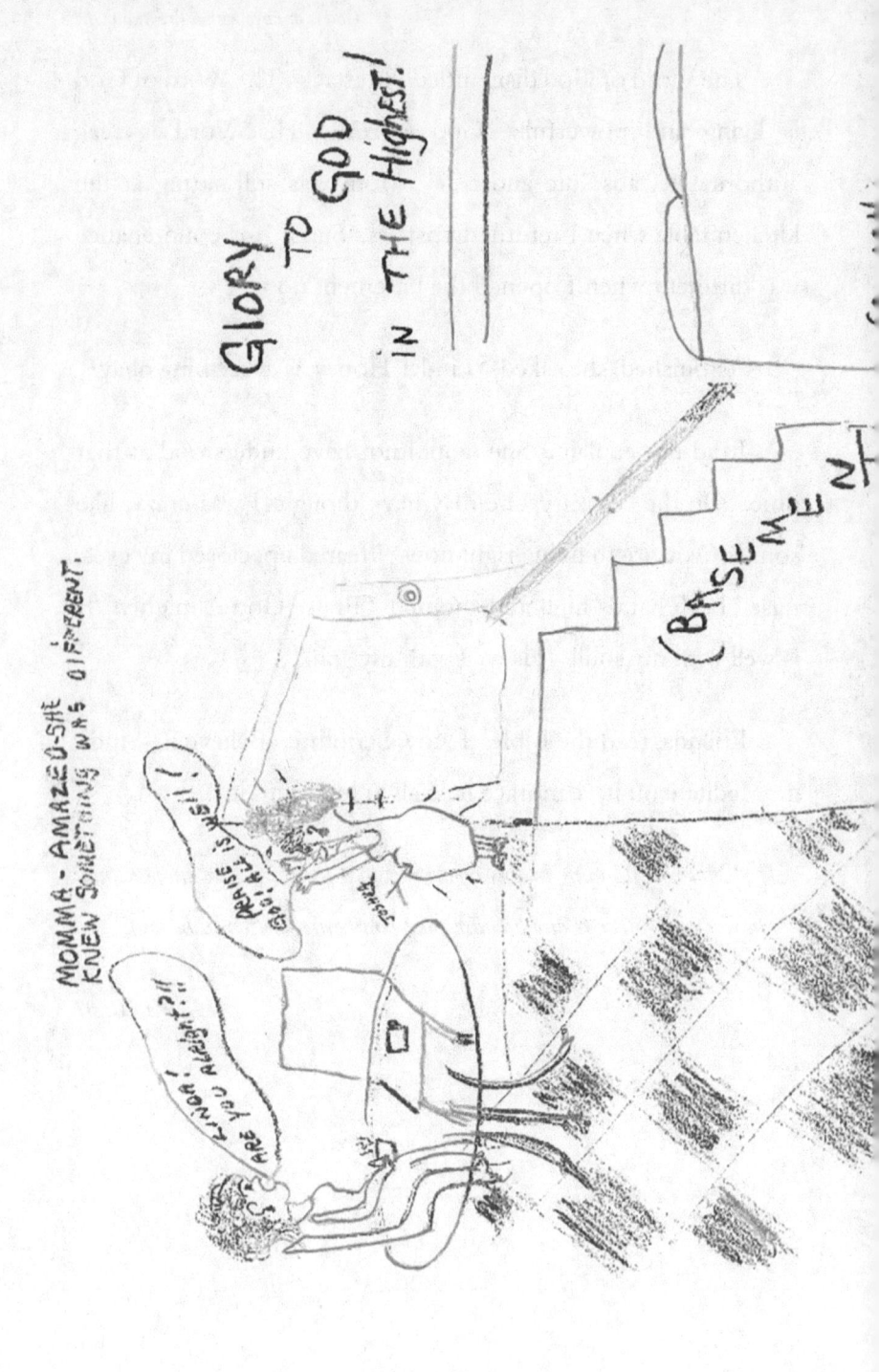

ENCOUNTER #6

MANY WATERS

I was feeling pretty good on this particular day. My dad sat in the family room watching television. "Good morning, Pop!" I said, happily breezing passed him.

"Hey sweetheart." He smiled and waved.

In the bathroom, I turned on my little radio and prepared to take a shower.

The baby inside kicked like crazy. I was glad about that. Then just like before, out of nowhere Satan began another ferocious mental attack. I was not in the same posture of strength. But God is always nearby to protect us for he is our Shepherd.

"I'm taking your mind!" Satan threatened, savagely.

"I'm going to kill that baby!"

"You can't! In Jesus Name! You can't!" I argued.

"You're a loser! What a low life! You're insane! Sinner!"

The thoughts were overwhelming coming so fast! I began to reel.

"Jesus! Help me!" I cried.

"Hypocrite!" He's not going to help you! You're nothing! Satan continued condemning me.

"He's left you all alone. You won't make it. Another child? Look at yourself! All this is too much for you! You're a worm! God hates you!"

The sudden, non-stop storm of blames literally took me to my knees. The prince of darkness of this world heaved accusations and threats to my mind like one endlessly firing an AR-15. Initially, I could not mentally configure a counter attack. I was caught off guard as it were. My mind was scrambled. I feared mental defeat. Unlike in my childhood when I had the stomach ache and was healed, this time I did not want to call for my dad. I had matured some in God's Word. My instinct was to fight. But I struggled for the battle plan

Besides, this wasn't about calling on the flesh. This was a spiritual battle. I knew I needed my Heavenly Father. I remembered that God called David a man after his own heart even though he committed adultery with Bathsheba and had her husband put on the front-line of war to be killed. I remembered how Jacob wasn't perfect but stole his father's blessing and was blessed. I remembered that God said he is the same, yesterday, today and forever! I remembered that he changes not! And I remembered *Psalms 91:15*.

"He shall call upon me, and I will answer him: I will be with him in trouble; I will deliver him, and honour him."

Now balled up on the floor, wrapped in a towel, I desperately called on the I AM THAT I AM! I began to open my mouth!

"My God! My God! My Father! My Lord! Come Lord! Come and help me now Father! Lord, please! Satan is trying to take my mind, Lord God!

"I own you!" Satan contended.

"Help me! Father, remove this attack in the Name of Jesus! I am your daughter, Father!"

"You're nobody! Your own family is ashamed of you!" Satan continued.

I kept talking to the Lord.

"God, you said to remind you of your Word. You said in your Word, that you would answer me when I call on you when I am in trouble.

"Loser!" The enemy persisted.

I screamed louder!

"I'm calling on you Lord God! Come now, Father! I need you now! I can't wait until the by and by or next week or tomorrow! Heavenly Father, was David any different than me? Do you love him more than me? Is Jacob any different than me? Do you love him more than me? If you are the God of Abraham, Isaac and Jacob and you are the same yesterday, today and forever, please come now and help me! You said that you change not! You helped Moses at the Red Sea, Lord! Help your daughter, Lord! Because of the blood of Jesus, I am your daughter, Lord God! Am I not washed in the blood of your Son, Jesus Christ? The devil is trying to take my mind, Lord! Save me! Please!"

While I cried out, the God of heaven heard my plea! As I prayed, the presence of the everlasting Father filled that bathroom! I sensed him straddled over me as I laid there balled up, my knees clinched to my chest. His powerful and commanding presence was defensive like a Shepherd protecting one of his sheep from a wolf. He came for me! Again, he came to me! He actually came to rescue me from my enemy! As I write this, I'm crying all over again to think that the God of the whole universe and everything in it, the One who made man from the dust of the ground, came to take care of little me. Me! I'm pregnant a second time, no husband, and he loves me…still.

The incursion ceased. My mind was regulated and restored with peace I have never known. My God is real! My God is powerful! My God loves his children! He will answer when we call out to him. He is so incredible! Guys, he loves you so very much. To him be praise, power and dominion now and forever. Amen.

"In my distress I called upon the Lord, and cried unto my God: he heard my voice out of his temple, and my cry came before him, even into his ears.

Then the earth shook and trembled; the foundations also of the hills moved and were shaken, because he was wroth.

There went up a smoke out of his nostrils, and fire out of his mouth devoured: coals were kindled by it.

He bowed the heavens also, and came down: and darkness was under his feet.

And he rode upon a cherub, and did fly: yea, he did fly upon the wings of the wind.

He made darkness his secret place; his pavilion round about him were dark waters and thick clouds of the skies. At the brightness that was before him his thick clouds passed, hail stones and coals of fire.

The Lord also thundered in the heavens, and the Highest gave his voice; hail stones and coals of fire.

Yea, he sent out his arrows, and scattered them; and he shot out lightning, and discomfited them.

Then the channels of waters were seen, and the foundations of the world were discovered at thy rebuke, O Lord, at the blast of the breath of thy nostrils.

He sent from above, he took me, he drew me out of many waters.

He delivered me from my strong enemy..."

Psalms 18: 6-17

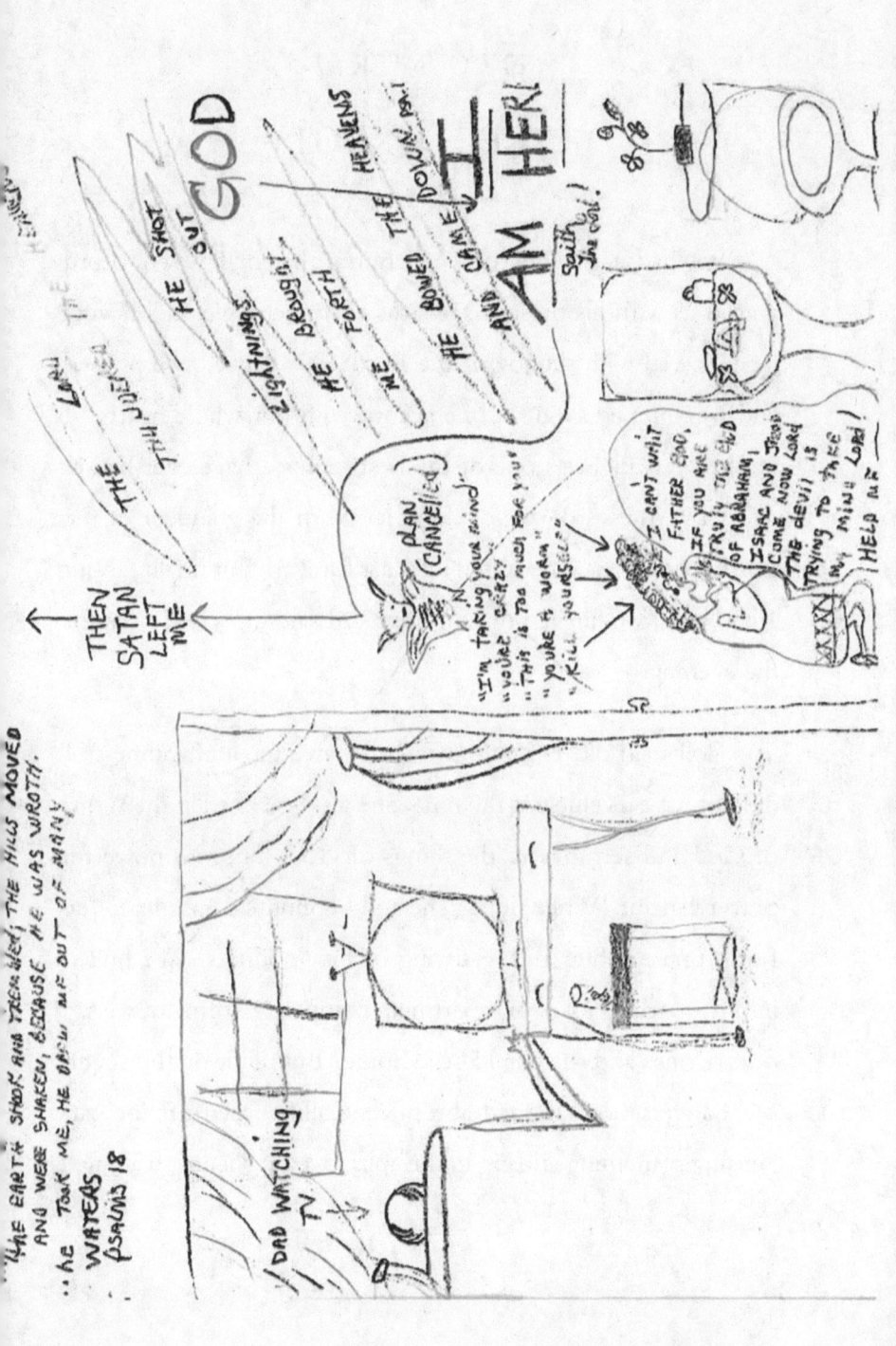

ENCOUNTER #7

TREE UPROOT

We had a glorious time at church that night. The Lord graced us with his presence. It was absolutely splendid! Every face glowed with the joy of the Lord. We danced, we praised and worshipped God on one accord with our whole hearts. I marked this night as one of the best nights I have ever had at church. Afterwards, we couldn't let go of the grandeur of the Lord's presence. We wanted it to last forever! But finally, about 10:30 p.m., we hugged one another and said our good-byes for the evening.

Collis, an older friend, offered to give me a lift home as I did not have a vehicle at the time. She was seasoned in the Word of God and sensitive to the things of God. She was powerful prayer warrior. While riding, she and I continued basking in the Lord, praising him and testifying of his goodness. We pulled into the parking lot at my apartment complex. Normally, we say our so longs and she would head home. But oddly on this night, our conversation stopped abruptly. Collis turned off the car. Sensing something stirring in the spirit, we sat silently, waiting.

After a moment or two, my flesh once again being suspended and ushered to the background, the Lord Jesus appeared in front of me. It was the back of him that I saw. I don't know if Collis saw him as I was seeing him, or if she even saw him at all. But she remained completely quiet and still as if she knew something was happening. Jesus bent down as if to sit.

He then backed into me in the L-shape sitting position just like I was sitting in the car seat. I was altogether beyond mesmerized! As with the swords, I was lifted into a state of deferment where my humanity took a back seat to my spirit. My physical eyes were wide-open in shear amazement. There were a cluster of trees that stood about 300 ft. in front of Collis's car. My focus was directed by the Lord to the tree in the middle. As I concentrated on that particular tree, the Lord gently spoke to my spirit saying,

"Tell it to uproot." My eyes opened even wider. I was petrified!

"Tell it to uproot? Me?" I questioned silently.

Collis remained totally still and not making a sound. I tried to process what was happening. I'm afraid to meet the order.

"But Lord, I can't tell a tree to uproot." I reasoned inside myself.

Jesus gently says again, "Tell it."

I thought about who it is that's telling me to do it. But I sat there frozen, intensely staring at the tree. I muttered choppy sound fragments, but no actual words came out. I began rationalizing within my flesh. I was thinking that, if that tree was uprooted because my very mouth told it to, I would have a heart attack. It would be more than I could handle. So, I resigned the thought of doing it. I did not say it because I allowed fear and human reasoning to get in the way of the command of the Lord. Afterwards, I told Collis what happened. I cried plentifully, begging God's forgiveness. She prayed for me and encouraged me not to condemn myself.

"The Lord knew you weren't going to tell the tree to uproot before he told you to. But he still chose you to know the power he has given us." She ministered.

I was so blessed! Jesus allowed me to realize the power of the Holy Spirit that lives within me, within us, within you, all the children of the Heavenly Father! Thank You Father God for such an amazing unforgettable experience! Thank you for revealing your power in the lives of those who belong to you. To you be glory, honor, praise, power and dominion forever!

"And the Lord said, if ye had faith as a grain of mustard seed, ye might say unto this sycamine tree, be thou plucked up by the root, and be thou planted in the sea; and it should obey you."

Luke 17:6

"Verily, verily, I say unto you, He that believeth on, the works that I do shall he do also; and greater works than these shall he do; because I go unto my Father."

John 14:12

I hope for another chance like that someday.
R.I.P. my dear friend, Collis.

ENCOUNTER #8

GEORGIA STATE UNIVERSITY/THE FLOOD WATERS

I prayed daily. I read a minimum of twenty Bible chapters every night, seeking God constantly and learning more about him.

I enrolled into Georgia State University to take some basic courses.

I was in the cafeteria having lunch with Pena, a classmate. I noticed a man a few tables across the room. I called her attention to him. We both could not help but notice his incredibly good looks. No argument there. But there was something else that stood out about him. I told Pena I'd be right back. I went over to him.

"Hello. My name is Linda." I said, with an extended hand.

He had a kind demeanor and was a perfect gentleman. He stood and introduced himself.

"Nice to meet you, Linda. I'm Charles." He said shaking my hand.

"Hey! Why don't you come to the Bible study that starts in fifteen minutes? It's in the Bass Hall conference room on the second floor."

"Ok! Yeah, sure!" I happily replied.

"Ah, Bible study!" I said to myself, rushing back to the table to gather my books.

"Pena, he invited me to a Bible study! It starts in fifteen minutes. I'm going! You want to come?"

"A Bible study? No, thanks."

I was so excited for the Bible study. By the time I got there Charles was already up at the podium preaching. I knew it! I knew there was something special about him. He preached from the Bible. Boy! He was on fire! I knew he spoke the truth, because he spoke things I had read in the Bible. At the end of the brief study, he invited those who wanted to give their hearts to the Lord to come down to the altar. Oh, I definitely wanted to! I was completely ready!

I rushed down towards him with my hands stretched towards heaven. He laid his hands on me and told me to begin praising God and thanking Him.

"Hallelujah! Hallelujah! Glory to God! Thank you, Jesus for dying for me! I love you, Lord! I praise you, Lord! You are worthy of praise, Lord!"

I continued praising the Lord with everything I had, with all my heart. Those around me mattered not. Nothing around me mattered. I blocked everything and everyone out of my mind. My focus was on God alone. I lost myself in praises to God. Praising him ushered me into his presence. I connected with God right there at the altar. Very humbled before the King, I began crying as I continued to lift up the Name of Jesus. I was before him. He is so holy, righteous, beautiful and perfect. Charles prayed over me and as at other times my spirit was illuminated, real, alive! I was again suspended in order to participate in the outpouring of the Holy Spirit! The Lord released spiritual torrential waters that gushed over my soul. It was an intensifying sound surpassing the powerful overflowing waters of Niagara Falls. My sins were being washed away! I'm telling you that it was an experience I'll never forget! I was being born again! Good God Almighty! I was being born again! He loves me! He loves you! He died for me! He died for you! He cleaned me! Has he cleaned you? I am His child. Are you? My second birth into the Spirit of God was at Georgia State University. Where was yours?

If you have not been born again by the Holy Spirit and do not have a reference place of your new birth in Jesus Christ, you can have one. Your experience may not be like mine, but it can be today! How? Repent today. Repent means to turn from the sin in your life. It means you choose Jesus Christ to rule and guide your life. He wants your heart. Make the decision to give it to him. Believe in him. Trust and allow him to guide your life. He will forgive your sins and give you eternal life! It doesn't matter about your past or what you are struggling with now. Give it all to him. He is waiting for you with open arms. He loves you!

"Come now, and let us reason together, saith the LORD: though your sins be as scarlet, they shall be as white as snow; though they be red like crimson, they shall be as white as snow; though they be red like crimson, they shall be as wool."

Isaiah 1:18

THE Holy Spirit Flooded my soul like OCEANS ARE BEING POURED OVER my soul.
GEORGIA STATE UNIVERSITY / CHAPEL
REPENT AFTER ME. HEAVENLY FATHER, FORGIVE ME FOR MY SINS. JESUS PLEASE COME INTO MY HEART AND HELP ME LIVE FOR YOU. NOW PRAISE God! PRAISE God!
HEAVENLY FATHER FORGIVE ME FOR MY SINS. JESUS PLEASE COME INTO MY HEART AND HELP ME LIVE FOR YOU!
REV. CHARLES
ME
"HALLELUYAH!"
"PRAISE the Lord!"
"I LOVE YOU, JESUS!"
"Glory to God!"
"BLESS THE LORD!"
HALLELUYAH! Glory To God!

ENCOUNTER #9

BALL OF FIRE

It was a beautiful day. The sun shone brightly. The wind was mildly perfect. It was a dry, clear 78-80 degrees. And boy, what a time we had at church that morning! I mean, it was like God had come down from heaven and literally sat among us! Our spirits were high, everyone rejoiced in his presence. We worshipped the Lord! Some so full, they just rocked back and forth in their seats. Others cried with raised hands, while some praised him in the dance. It was beautiful! On the way home, Mary Grace, another dear friend and I continued to bask in God's love, beauty and power. She dropped me off at my place. I went inside, helped my daughter get into play clothes to go outside with her friends.

I was still so full. I could hardly contain myself. I wanted to praise God more. I wanted to stay in that posture and worship God forever. I pushed back the curtains in my daughter's bedroom just to look outside and see his earthly and heavenly landscape. I could strongly sense his presence. I knelt down beside her bed. With my hands lifted I began worshipping the King. With my eyes shut, I became engulfed in his praise. The outside world began to fade. My total and complete attention was on the Lord. I was right there with him, one with him and he with me. He was all that was important. He was my single focus. Then, just like before, I was lifted. The best way I can describe it is, my spirit became the dominant part of me. My soul and body were secondary. In this hung state, I gazed at the heavens. Suddenly, there appeared before me a ball of fire. I'm blown away! Initially, it was about the size of a large beach ball. Smaller flames sparked from all around it, like a miniature sun. Slowly it turned, moving towards me. The closer it came to me, the smaller it became. It was reduced to the size of a basketball, and then a softball and finally, about the size of an orange. The petite fiery ball continued in slow motion. Tiny, energetic sparks continued bouncing from it. I'm like a statue, watching this! It came nearer to my face. But just before it reached me, it unraveled in a circular activity, remaining very, very much alive. It was like peeling an orange in one piece in a rounded motion with no breaks. The end of the unraveled blaze took on a finger-like form and touched my lips! I began speaking in other tongues! My spirit soared! This is beyond beautiful! I spoke in tongues for several minutes. In the language, I sensed I was still praising God and with my complete self and with everything I had. I then bowed my head and cried heavily because he is so very amazing! I was humbled. I also cried because the God who created everything, knows everything, would visit me in such a powerful way. Me? Me? Why? A wretch, saved by his grace. He will visit you. Love him. Worship him with your whole heart. No matter what you may be going through, worship him. Call until he comes. I promise you that he will come to you.

"Call unto me, and I will answer thee and shew thee great and mighty things, which thou knowest not."

Jeremiah 33:3

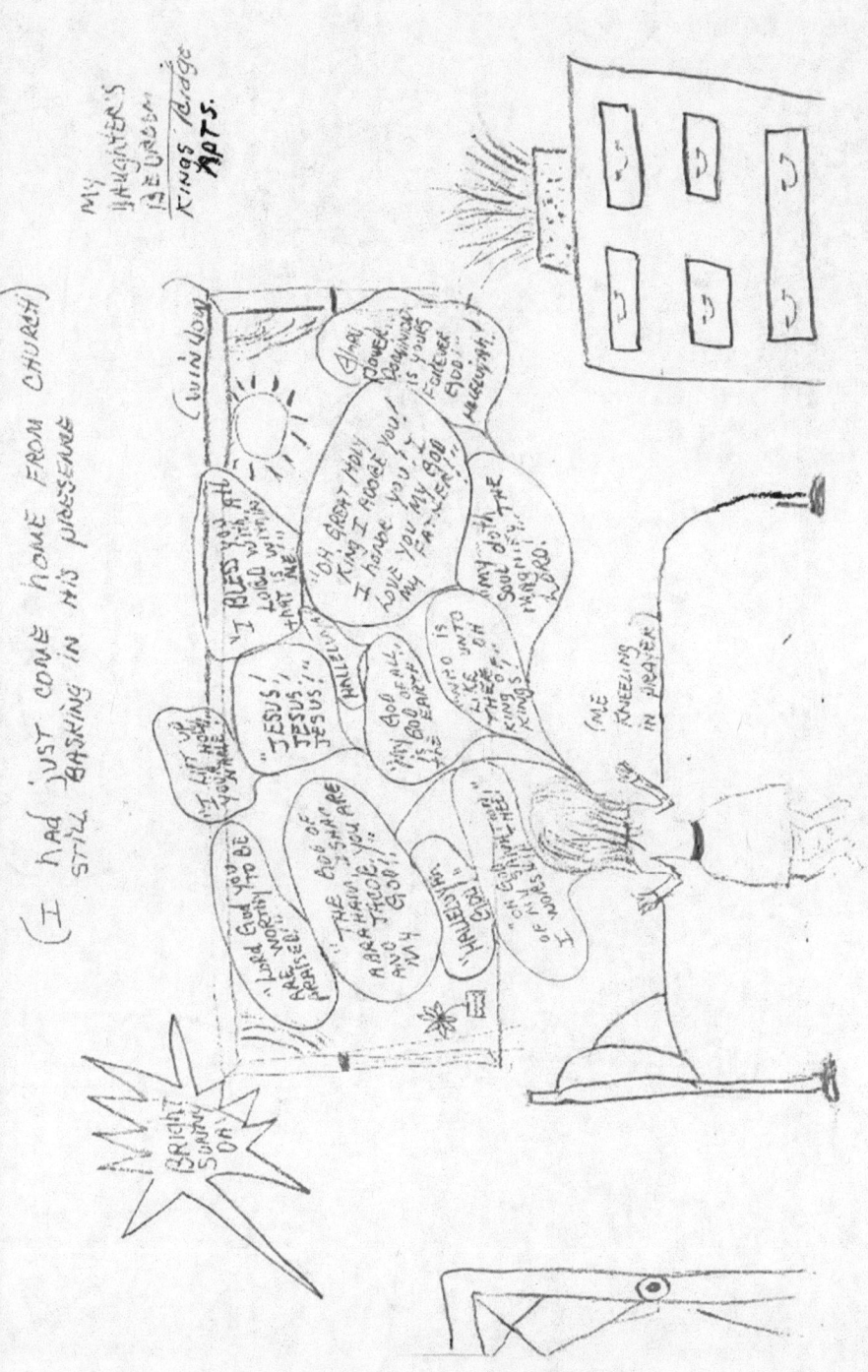

ENCOUNTER #10

SYMPHONY OF THE PSALMS

My Bible reading and prayer time was done mostly late at night after I had gotten the kids off to bed. Each night, I anointed their foreheads and their feet, asking the Lord to always keep them with the mind of Christ and to order their footsteps.

It was a quiet late night. A good time to go into the presence of the Lord while the world was still. I was reading the Psalms. I would stop reading occasionally to soak in and ponder a verse that I had just read. Various portions of the book of Psalms at different times, tells of God's vastness, his inexhaustibleness, his beauty, his power, his wisdom, his perfection, his sovereignty, his counsel, his judgments and his love.

"How precious also are thy thoughts unto me, O God! How great is the sum of them? If I should count them, they are more in number than the sand: when I awake, I am still with thee."

Psalms 139:17 & 18

Think about this! I mean, really think about the words that God is speaking here! Every word of this verse gives me confidence in this world. How precious are his thoughts toward me (and you) that they outnumber the sand! The sand? That is a love that is incomprehensible! Knowing that I have the love of the Almighty God backing me, the One who spoke the universe into being, whom shall I fear?

I was lying in bed relishing his Word. The book of Psalms is simply beautiful. It's poetic. But more importantly, it's alive! I was one with every word of it. There were no distractions. No television on. No radio. No movement. Not a sound. The world meant nothing to me at the time. My troubles were afar off. My soul was so full I could burst. My God was there with me. I could sense his presence. Tears of wonderment, joy and awe filled my eyes as I wholly embraced and considered the words of the above scripture.

As at other times, I was shifted into the Spirit. I began hearing a phenomenal sound. My God! *Is that music?* I think to myself. Yes, it was music! It swept into my spirit ever so sweetly. I was still as a statue. Yes! It was indeed, music! Heavenly music! Music like I had never heard before! I likened it to a symphony. I listened in shear amazement to this indescribable, soft angelic music. It was the purest melodic sounds I've ever heard! There is no opus man can ever produce that could compare to it. I was totally and completely astonished at what I was hearing! God is allowing me to hear his heavenly orchestra! I'm tearing up as I write this, thinking of his love for me, for you. I do not know why he loves us this way, but I am so glad he does!

All he wants is for us to obey him, love him, trust and believe in him as a child does a father. He has great, great wonders to share with us. Things we cannot fathom, he wants to share with us, far beyond the realm of this world. There is a God-given power that we as the children of God can tap into if we give him our whole hearts. He wants our hearts, all of it. Ninety-nine and a half won't do. Do it! I guarantee that you won't be disappointed.

"But as it is written, eye hath not seen, nor ear heard, neither have entered into the heart of man, the things which God hath prepared for them that love him."

1 Corinthians 2:9

"Whom having not seen, ye love; in whom, though now ye see him not, yet believing, ye rejoice with joy unspeakable and full of glory;"

1 Peter 1:8

ENCOUNTER #11

NAME THE CHILD

I'm pregnant with my second child. I still attended church pretty much every time the doors opened. I also continued daily my personal Bible study. My daughter and I had gone through a lot. Low-income housing, barely surviving and many related circumstances I waded through with the help of the Lord. No matter what came my way, good or bad, I trusted in Jesus Christ.

My daughter came home after school one day, telling me that one of her classmates was named, Blessed. I thought, *wow*, what a wonderful name. I hoped the child I was carrying would be blessed and that my whole family would be blessed. I wanted to be surprised at the sex of the child, therefore refused to have an ultrasound. I decided that Blessed would be the name of my child whichever sex it was. Yes, Blessed!

After getting my daughter to bed, I took a shower and prepared to unwind and read my Bible. I got into bed with the Bible open on my large belly. Normally, I'd pick up where I left off, or read the Psalms, my favorite book. But this particular night, I wanted the Lord to give me what to read. So, I asked him what he would like me to read. The night was still and quiet.

Blocking all other thoughts, I waited silently in his presence for an answer. I thought he may say, "Read Matthew." Or direct me to "Genesis." Or one of the other books of the Bible. Although it was not the answer I was expecting, he did speak softly saying,

"Name the child, Joshua."

I sat straight up in bed. I had to process what he had just said to me.

"Name the child, Joshua. Name the child, Joshua! Joshua!" I proclaimed!

"Oh my gosh! I'm having a boy! His name will be, Joshua!"

Early the next morning, I called my friend Mary Grace, who rejoiced and praised God with me. I must have told this incredible true story to my son at least one-hundred times, I know. I want him to always remember that he was named by God himself! And that God gave him his very own Name. I tell him that Jesus, Yeshua and Joshua all mean Jehovah is my salvation! Every time someone says his name, Joshua, they declare that Jehovah is salvation! What an honor! The Lord God named my son!

When we have a true and strong relationship with the Lord, we can ask him anything with the right heart and he will answer us. What do you want to ask the Lord? Go ahead, ask him Don't get up so quickly when you pray. Wait there in his presence for his answer. Stay one with him. Believe. He will answer. And if he doesn't answer right away, continue to ask with your whole heart. He will answer you. Be patient.

"Ask, and it shall be given you; seek, and ye shall find; knock, and it shall be opened unto you. For everyone that asketh receiveth; and he that seeketh findeth; and to him that knocketh it shall be opened."

Mathew 7: 7 & 8

GOD SPOKE TO MY HEART

"NAME THE CHILD JOSHUA"

(I hadn't had an ultrasound to determine the baby's sex)

BEDTIME
KING'S RIDGE APTS.
ATLANTA, GA

HEAVENLY FATHER, PLS GUIDE ME WHAT TO SPEAK TONIGHT. SPEAK TO MY HEART LORD, I'M OPEN TO HEAR YOUR VOICE FATHER SPEAK TO ME. IN JESUS' NAME.

BIBLE

ENCOUNTER #12

I AM WITH THEE ALWAYS

"Whither shall I go from thy spirit? or whither shall I flee from thy presence? If I ascend up into heaven, thou art there: if I make my bed in hell, behold, thou art there. If I take the wings of the morning, and dwell in the uttermost parts of the sea; Even there shall thy hand lead me, and thy right hand shall hold me."

Psalms 139: 7-10

Daily, I juggled the taxing duties of a single mother of now three children. I was mother, father, teacher, counselor, doctor, referee, housekeeper, mediator, cook, provider, encourager, disciplinarian, minister, transportation coordinator, hair dresser, hygienist and director of recreation. I also managed my son's singing career with hopes of getting us all out of poverty. At that time food stamps were issued in colored paper dollar bills. Coin change was only given from the pink one-dollar bills. I needed to get enough change to buy non-food items such as soap, toilet paper, deodorant, etc. Using the pink one-dollar bills, I walked to various mom-and-pop stores in the area to buy a .25 pack of chewing gum or a piece of candy. Getting .75 change back from each purchase I used the money for the non-food items we needed. Wearing so many hats took its toll on me over time. Daily woes besieged me to the point where I nearly had a nervous breakdown. I once left the house, walking out into pouring down rain to keep from losing it, or perhaps snapping on the kids. Another time, I suddenly grabbed a man who was walking near me and breaking down to him, crying. I was getting into a serious mental danger zone. I needed to talk to someone.

I endured a three week stay in a local mental hospital diagnosed as being "Severely Depressed". My oldest daughter, sixteen at the time, cared for my two younger children during my hospital stay. While there getting the help I needed, I stayed quietly in my room reading my Bible seventy-five percent of the time. I was astonished that patients visited my room for me to share the Bible with them. God used me in the hospital. To my surprise, some stayed in my room for over an hour, just sharing. It was great to be used of God in that way, but when I came home, there was still that one guy for whom I was weak in the flesh. The following and final encounter is a really tough one, but I am hoping someone will find hope in this incredible testimonial.

I found out I was pregnant...again. Another baby? I simply couldn't do it. A fourth child? Mentally and emotionally, I just could not do it. I know, you must be saying, "Really? Why didn't you use protection?" It's ok. I asked myself that, too. I thought I had grown strong enough to abstain. But obviously, I had not. I loved the guy. Or at least I thought I did. I thought I could keep him away. I had dismissed him several times, but he would sweet talk his way back into my life. I didn't use protection because I aimed to stand on God's Word and live my life accordingly. But my flesh had always been a huge challenge ever since my teenage years. My flesh was weak.

So, I was now at a huge crossroad. Will I keep the baby or not? In the sight of God, I couldn't believe I was even considering an abortion. An abortion? Me? I shuttered at the thought of it. I was a complete wreck, wrestling back and forth with my decision every day, all day long. I wasn't sleeping. I was not eating well and lacked good hygiene. I could not handle a fourth child. I was already a hair away from a permanent stay in the mental hospital in trying to raise the three that I had. I prayed earnestly. I begged God's forgiveness. On my knees I sobbed heavily each and every night, sometimes until I fell asleep.

"Father, please forgive me. I have sinned against you and you only."

For nearly three weeks I prayed for him to say something about my situation. Anything? I would even accept his rebuke.

I just wanted him to say something. There was no one else to talk to or to help like he could. I knew that without him, I was nothing. I continued to bombard heaven.

"Father, whatever you decide it will be just and so be it. Like David, I said, "Just don't take your Spirit away from me." Who else can I turn to, Lord? Who else do I have? You said that you would throw my sin in the sea of forgetfulness, Father. Does this sin get thrown into the sea of forgetfulness too, Lord? I'm so sorry, Lord. I have gone my own way, but I have no one but you, Lord. Just don't leave me, Lord. Please just don't leave me, Jesus. I deserve whatever punishment you see fit for me, Lord God but, say something Father. Speak to me. Say something! Anything! Help me. I really do want to please you. I want to be free of fornication, Lord. I can't do it by myself, Lord. You said, the blood of Jesus covers our sins. Does it not cover this one too, Lord? Forgive me Father. I know I have hurt your heart yet again. I am sorry, Lord. Please have mercy on me. Deliver me, Father. Help me to live for you with my whole being."

I only knew one thing. And that was I am nothing without Jesus Christ.

Day after day, I continued praying. I heard nothing from the Lord. But I continued to pray and beg his forgiveness. One morning about 2:30 am, he visited me as I slept. I was yanked from sleep. More like pushed, if you will. I sensed the Lord was angry with me. Can you imagine Almighty God being angry with you? It is most terrifying!

"Get up!" He conveyed to my spirit.

Greatly humbled and thankful for the visit, I rolled quickly out of bed onto the floor on my knees, head bowed. I literally quivered in his presence feeling guilty, ashamed and afraid.

"Yes Lord." I answered, trembling.

"Read the account where David numbered the people." He instructed.

His presence then lifted.

Thankful for the visit and instruction, I turned on the light and picked up my Bible. Flipping nervously through the pages, I found the account in the Bible in 2 Samuel, chapter 24 when David numbered the people of Israel. God had specifically instructed him not to number the people. David counted the people anyway. God was displeased. He sent Gad the prophet to speak to David regarding his wrongdoing. God offered David three choices of punishment from which he was to choose:

"Go and say unto David, thus saith the Lord, I offer thee three things; choose thee one of them, that I may do it unto thee. So Gad came to David, and told him, and said unto him, Shall seven years of famine come unto thee in thy land? or wilt thou flee three months before thine enemies, while they pursue thee? or that there be three days' pestilence in thy land? now advise, and see what answer I shall return to him that sent me.

And David said unto Gad, I am in a great strait: let us fall now into the hand of the Lord; for his mercies are great: and let me not fall into the hand of man.

So, the Lord sent a pestilence upon Israel from the morning even to the time appointed: and there died of the people from Dan even to Beersheba seventy thousand men."

2 Samuel 24: 12-15

From reading that account, I believed that I was to decide my own punishment. I reluctantly chose to proceed with the abortion and hope for the mercies of God. My choice plagued me every day, all day. On the morning of the 6:00 a.m. scheduled procedure, I was up at 3:00 a.m., praying.

"Father, if it is your will to end my life as it relates to this procedure, please allow me to make it back home first. I don't want my children to have to say their mother died while having an abortion. I ask for your mercy, Lord. I have no one but you."

With unspeakable remorse and sorrow, I set up my communion table. I held up the cup towards heaven. With tears that seemed to carry with them pieces of my soul, I said to my Father, "I am most unworthy Lord, but is this not the reason you came into the world, Lord? Do you no longer love me? Am I cast out? Don't cast me away, my Lord. I beg you, don't leave me please! And if it is death you decide for me, please let me know that I am still yours and receive me home."

Shaking, I took the bread and held it up.

"Oh, King of Glory. This is your body. The covenant of the New Testament. Am I no longer a part of the body of Christ? You said if we sin, we have an advocate, Jesus Christ the righteous. I beseech you Father, honor your word and forsake me not, Lord. Please have mercy on me."

A close friend drove me to the appointment. We arrived 20 minutes early. I am placed in a room where I am left alone to get changed into a hospital gown and lie down on the bed. When the nurse entered, I never spoke a word to her or anyone. I nervously sat up shaking my head, no. My out-of-control trembling signaled my spiritual, mental and emotional discomfort with my decision. Gently touching my shoulder, the nurse ushered me back down on to the bed.

"Everything will be okay. Don't worry." She said, trying to comfort me.

I continue shaking my head back and forth in opposition. I'm thinking, "Lady, you don't understand. This is against my Father. I'm scared. I don't know if I can do this."

Nearly in shock, unable to speak, I again sat up shaking my head, no.

"Try and relax, dear." She said, guiding the top half of my body back down on to the bed.

Yet again, I sat up quivering and shaking my head.

"Sweetheart, I promise you're going to be okay."

And once more, she gently ushered me down on to the bed and left the room. My teeth were banging together, I'm shuddering badly. With tears running down my face, I manage to whisper to the Lord.

"You said in your Word that your mercies are new every morning. Are they new for me on this morning? Please extend your new morning mercies for me today, Father."

It was then that the presence of my loving, merciful, forgiving heavenly Father entered the room and said these words to me:

"Lo, I am with thee always; even unto the end of the world."

Matthew 28:20

On an abortion table, he comforted his child. He came to see about me. As horrible and detestable as the situation was, he came. I have no words that can ever fully express the

magnitude of God's mercy. I am forever grateful. And my baby? I will see the child. Not in this life, but in the next. I am reminded of David who said of his baby who passed away,

"...I shall go to him, but he shall not return to me."

2 Samuel 12:23

Satan was sure of my demise that time. He thought he had finally finished me.

"But God, who is rich in mercy, for his great love wherewith he loved us,"

Ephesians 2:4

The Great Shepherd will always protect his flock. God is never pleased with our sin. But the heart that repents, he will in no way cast out. There is forgiveness in the heart of God through Jesus Christ! Come to him. Bring Jesus your sin and lay it at his feet.

> *"My little children, these things write I unto you, that ye sin not. And if any man sin, we have an advocate with the Father, Jesus Christ the righteous:"*
>
> 1 John 2:1

"Come now, and let us reason together, though your sins be as scarlet, they shall be as white as snow; though they be red like crimson, they shall be as wool."

Isaiah 1:18

Just as newborns cry for help for want of feeding and diaper changes, and toddlers who stumble and fall and cry for help from their parents, we as children in the Lord do the same. We stumble and fall as well. However, we are to grow in Christ by praying and studying his Word. But, whenever we cry out to the Heavenly Father with a true repentant heart, he picks us up and helps us continue on our journey in him. God knows we are not perfect. He knows we are but dust, for he made us. And yet he gave his life for us. He loves us in spite of our sin.

"While we were yet sinners, Christ died for us."

Romans 5:8

Beloved, please know that God loves you exactly the way you are. He sees you every day. He knows what you're doing and what you are feeling. He wants you to repent (turn away from the sin in your life). Make him Lord of your life. Call on him. Invite him into your heart. Learn of him by reading his Word. Ask for his forgiveness for transgression of his law and he will give you a love that you have never known. And that love will last for all eternity!

"For God so loved the world that he gave his only begotten Son, that whosoever believeth in him shall not perish, but have everlasting life."

John 3:16

"That if thou shalt confess with thy mouth the Lord Jesus, and shalt believe in thine heart that God hath raised him from the dead, thou shall be saved."

Romans 10:9

"Greater love hath no man than this, that a man lay down his life for his friends."

John 15:13

To the only wise God our Saviour, be glory and majesty, dominion and power both now and forever. Amen.

Jude 25

Love

Thank you, Jesus! Thank you, Jesus! Thank you, Jesus!

www.ingramcontent.com/pod-product-compliance
Lightning Source LLC
LaVergne TN
LVHW030344070526
838199LV00067B/6445